A CHRISTMAS LONGING

JONI EARECKSON TADA

MULTNOMAH BOOKS

SISTERS, OREGON

To my art teacher, James Sewell…from your grateful student.

A CHRISTMAS LONGING

published by Multnomah Books, a part of the Questar publishing family

©1990, 1996 by Joni Eareckson Tada
International Standard Book Number: 1-57673-024-7
(previously 0-88070-366-0)

Edited by Larry Libby, Design by David Uttley (D² DesignWorks)
Printed in the United States of America

Unless otherwise noted, Scripture quotations are from:

The Holy Bible, New International Version (NIV) ©1973, 1984 by International Bible Society,
used by permission of Zondervan Publishing House

Also quoted:*New American Standard Bible* (NASB) ©1960, 1977 by the Lockman Foundation

The King James Version (KJV)

The New Testament in Modern English, Revised Edition (Phillips) ©1972 by J. B. Phillips

For information:
Questar Publishers, Inc. • Post Office Box 1720 • Sisters, Oregon 97759

LIBRARY OF CONGRESS CATALOGING-IN-PUBLICATION DATA:

Tada, Joni Eareckson.
A christmas longing/ Joni Eareckson Tada.
p. cm.
ISBN 0-88070-366-0
1. Christmas—Meditations. 2. Jesus Christ—
Meditations I. Title
BV45.T32   1990
242′.33—dc20   90-35692 CIP

96 97 98 99 00 01 02 03 — 10 9 8 7 6 5 4 3 2 1

CONTENTS

INTRODUCTION

Rummaging through our garage one December afternoon, I sniffed the unmistakable fragrance of new leather. From that moment, Santa Claus was dethroned from my childhood.

There it was behind a box—a new pony bridle.

That was it. No more 7-Up and cookies left on the mantelpiece on Christmas Eve. No more bleeding-heart letters to the North Pole. No more sugar for the reindeer. Carrots, either. I was relieved. Something deep down told me it had all been a ploy, anyway. That's when Christmas became more…serious. No, not somber. Just more important.

I was only seven years old, but from then on, it was clear that December 25 was a special day. A holy day. The candlelight Christmas Eve service at our Reformed Episcopal Church had new and deeper meaning. Almost overnight, Christmas Eve became one of those "silent nights" to ponder the miracle of Jesus.

The sanctuary was dark but oh so warm. Up and down each pew, a candle was passed to light the one we held in our hands. When mine was lit, I held it tightly, staring into the flame. I felt as though I were holding something holy. When I leaned on the kneelers to pray, I tried to make my prayer last as long as the little candle, as though that would be proof of my heart's desire that this be an important night. I wanted Jesus to know how special I thought He was.

And pray I did, long and earnest. But as I sat back into the pew, I expected something else to happen. Something to fill that strange longing inside of me.

After church was over, we crunched across the snowy parking lot to our car. I looked up into the night sky, spotted a bright star, and naively asked my father, "Is that the same star that was over the manger?" I was disappointed at his answer, but that didn't stop me from gazing at the star.

When we returned home, Mother prepared a tray of breads and cold cuts for our annual midnight Christmas Eve open house. I sat on the couch in our darkened living room between Aunt Dorothy and Aunt Helen, listening to Christmas music on the radio. Candles glowed in the window. Snow fell softly outside. Mother came in to serve late-night tea (I was astounded that she allowed me to stay up until such an hour).

I kept waiting for something to happen as the hour drew nearer to midnight. But what was I waiting for?

I fell asleep long before my aunts and uncles went home, and the next morning I would have said it was all a dream. That same dreamy nostalgia carried over throughout Christmas Day. I knew, as a child, I was free to play with my new toys and gifts all afternoon, but something in my seven-year-old heart would not allow me to spend Christmas Day self-absorbed. Several times during the morning—and even that afternoon—I left my gifts, went up to my room, and leaned on the windowsill to gaze outside.

What was I looking for? Why did I feel this mysterious pull to get away, go beyond, even "step into the other side" of Christmas?

Bright red ribbons, scented pine branches, spices and candles, the softness of falling snow, twinkling lights, the joy and laughter—these things were warm and precious, but they also were inklings, hints and whispers of an even greater celebration. *A celebration to come.*

I know now that I was deep into a Christmas longing. It's a longing each of us senses this time of year—especially when we listen to the child inside of us. It's a desire to be home, to belong, to find fulfillment, complete and eternal. Christmas is an invitation to a celebration yet to happen.

On this side of eternity, Christmas is still a promise. Yes, the Savior has come, and with Him peace on earth, but the story is not finished. Yes, there is peace in our hearts, but we long for peace in our world.

Every Christmas is still a "turning of the page" until Jesus returns.

Every December 25 marks another year that draws us closer to the fulfillment of the ages, that draws us closer to…Home.

Every holiday carol is a beautiful echo of the heavenly choir which will one day fill the universe with joy and singing.

Each Christmas gift is a foreshadowing of our gifts of golden crowns to be cast at the feet of the King of kings.

Each smile, each embrace beckons us onward, calls us upward when we will be with loved ones forever, when we will see our Lord face to face.

Angels hovering over treetops may have heralded His birth in the Bethlehem night, but one day they will herald the dawning of the new day. The glow of each candle is but a flicker compared to the Light by which "the nations will walk and the kings of the earth will bring their splendor."

There's a name for that kind of nostalgia, and, as a child, I may have even recognized it had someone told me.

It's a Christmas longing.

Joni Eareckson-Tada, paralyzed in a 1967 diving accident,
painted these pictures holding pencils and brushes between her teeth.
God has become the answer to her deepest longings and
she expresses this with every illustration.

God is the answer to our deepest longings.

1 CORINTHIANS 6:13
(PHILLIPS)

The First Advent . . .

AN AWAKENED

LONGING

Nevertheless, there will be no more gloom

for those who were in distress.

In the past he humbled the land of Zebulun

and the land of Naphtali,

but in the future he will honor Galilee of the Gentiles,

by the way of the sea, along the Jordan—

ISAIAH 9:1

"But you, Bethlehem Ephrathah,

though you are small among the clans of Judah,

out of you will come for me one who will be ruler over Israel,

whose origins are from of old,

from ancient times."

MICAH 5:2

Imagine walking through your front door and inhaling the mouth-watering aroma of Christmas turkey roasting in the oven. You heard you were having a stuffed bird for holiday dinner, but now it's here. Your "sniffer" tells you so.

Well…not quite. That drumstick will spend another hour in the oven before you lift it to your mouth. Dinner is not ready yet. It's time…almost. Funny thing is, you didn't know you were hungry before you walked into the house. The sweet aroma did it.

That's the nature of things that "whet your appetite." And this is why we look back at Jesus' birth with such longing. We never knew how hungry we were for God until Jesus arrived. When He was delivered onto the stable straw, we caught the fragrance of the presence of God. We inhaled the aroma of "God with us" and became acutely aware of a hunger deep inside. We hardly had words for it, but it was…it *is* a longing for the Lord.

For those who embrace the Savior in their heart's stable, God has given the Spirit as a guarantee, a down payment, or more in line with turkey dinners, He has "whetted our appetite." He is here within us; but He is still coming. His kingdom has arrived, but not in its fullness. And so we look back to the First Advent with warm pleasure… we cradle the Lord Jesus in our hearts…we breathe in the sweet-smelling savor of His presence…and treasure the time when soon, very soon, we shall sit down with Him at the banquet.

Until then, we look back at Bethlehem, smile, and…thank Him for giving us a taste of glorious things to come.

A CHRISTMAS LOOK

Christmas is a time for looking up… Looking up at a blanket of stars. Looking with joy into the night sky, dreaming of what it must have been like to see the Bethlehem star. Look up and marvel at the starry expanse above you. *God* came down from there! God left His heaven in order to best love you. Christmas is the time for looking up and remembering that heaven is your home.

Christmas is a time for looking down… Searching into your heart, recognizing the Christ-child within you, thanking Him for His Spirit which resides within. Christmas is the time for looking down and recognizing the need to kindle anew your own lamp of love, that its flame may burn ever more brightly.

Christmas is a time for looking around… Sharing smiles with friends, gifts for those we love. Look around at the needs of the people God brings your way. Christmas is the time to be the hands of God, touching the hungry, the homeless, those who are lonely, and all those who need your love, His love.

But *Christmas is also a time for looking ahead…* A new year is just around the corner, packed full of opportunities to witness for Him, to share His gospel of peace. Look ahead and dream. Plan and prepare. Be courageous, be bold. The future is an open door ready for you to walk through.

But most of all, *Christmas is a time for looking back…* Do that today, won't you? Look

back reverently across the centuries to the stable in Bethlehem. Picture the scene. Enter the village. Feel the crisp night air. See your frosty breath and feel the crunch of the gravel as you walk the path toward the inn. Stop at its door and listen to the laughter inside. Now step around the corner to the back of the inn and pause before the stable. Smell the fragrance of hay and straw. Let the warm glow of the stable lantern touch your face. Hear the cry of a tiny infant. Now wait and listen…hear the distant strains of singing angels.

Step inside the stable and marvel at what you see. Draw near, come close. Don't be afraid. This is the Lord of the universe come down to be with…you. In your heart, kneel before your Lord. Come worship and adore Him.

Why? Because *Christmas is a time for looking at the Lord Jesus.*

CHRISTMAS BILLBOARDS

Bombarded as we are by radio jingles, slick TV ads, splashy newspaper inserts, and dazzling store displays, we need to work at staying single-minded about the meaning of Christmas.

We know that Jesus entered human history quietly on a cold winter's night in a dark little stable. There were no jingles, billboards, or glitzy television commercials to advertise His advent.

But that's not to say His coming was unannounced.

God certainly did advertise the coming of His Son long before His birth. Christ's entry into the human family was the culmination of a long line of prophetic statements. Genesis describes Him as "the Seed" of the woman. Numbers calls Him both "Star" and "Scepter." Job pictures Him as the "Redeemer." Song of Solomon calls Him "the Rose of Sharon." Isaiah reveals Him as "the Servant" of God. Jeremiah names Him "the Lord Our Righteousness," and Daniel, "the Messiah." In Haggai, He is the "Desire of all nations." In Zechariah, "the King." In Malachi, "the Messenger of the Covenant."

Billboards. Signposts. And there were more. The city where Jesus would be born; the heralding work of John the Baptist; the journey into Egypt; descriptions of His ministry, His betrayal, His agonizing death on the cross, and His resurrection—all were foretold in graphic detail.

When you look back on these Old Testament billboards, you wonder how anyone could have *missed* the coming of Messiah on that winter night. Yet so many did. In spite of all those advertisements, people did miss Him. Most were either indifferent or blind to the amazing fact that God Himself intervened in human history. Even though there seemed to be an air of feverish expectation by the time Christ was actually born, most folks just failed to read the signs.

It reminds me of a story I once heard about a woman who lived alone in the hills of the South. In her great mansion she had many pictures of her hero, Robert E. Lee. One night in a snowstorm, two men stopped at her house for temporary shelter. She fed them and provided a place for them to rest. Upon leaving, one of the men, who was very distinguished in appearance, gave her a little gift. The woman became curious and asked the other man the name of her gentlemanly guest.

"That, ma'am," he replied, "is General Robert E. Lee." Before she could speak, they were gone. She had missed her chance to meet the one who had meant so much to her. And although she had his pictures all over the walls of her living room, she failed to recognize him when he came.

Maybe that's what happened the night Jesus arrived. Perhaps the people had preconceived notions about this Messiah of theirs. Certainly they were up on their prophecy. But it obviously took more than just reading the signposts. As in that story, it took more than just hanging up a few pictures.

People then and people today need to look for the *Person*. Not simply a title, a label, a piece of prophecy, or a name. The Son of God is a Person. And today, much like those days nearly two thousand years ago, we must not miss our chance to meet this marvelous Person, the Lord Jesus.

Could it be that you've looked past the signs? In all the materialistic media hype, could it be that you've somehow failed to notice His coming…His nearness?

The whole Bible is built around the story of Christ and His promise of life everlasting to men. The signs are there that we might believe and understand, know and love and follow Him.

How Can This Be?

Once upon a time, in a galaxy far, far away, an angel left on a journey.

He soared across the paths of suns and stars and entered another galaxy, a very special galaxy. The angel crossed one solar system after another, past spinning planets, to one certain, specific planet. He entered earth's atmosphere, crossing oceans, to a barren land in an obscure corner of the world.

It was here the angel arrived at a little town called Nazareth. He flew down streets and alleys to a certain home. Here, his journey across space and time ended. The angel had crossed a universe to stop in front of a dusty little house on a side street in a small village on the edge of a desert.

Across eternity and innumerable light years, the angel had come. His message was for neither king nor prince. Caesar was unaware of the visitation. Herod would know soon enough. The angel had been sent to speak to a peasant girl—a young, ordinary girl sitting on the edge of her bed in her room in that dusty little house. The angel entered, appeared, and spoke. The words he uttered to the girl were simple and direct. They were startling words which sent shock waves across the galaxies.

"Greetings, you who are highly favored!" the angel said to her. "The Lord is with you.... Do not be afraid, Mary, you have found favor with God. You will be with child and give birth to a son, and you are to give him the name Jesus. He will be great and will be called the Son of the Most High. The Lord God will give him the throne of his father David, and he will reign over the house of Jacob forever; his kingdom will never end" (Luke 1:28, 30–33).

Artists have tried for ages to capture that moment on canvas. Poets have pondered it. Dreamers have wondered about it. We can only guess what that young peasant girl named Mary must have done. Did she clutch her blanket? Did she hide behind a pillow on her bed as any teenager might do? Did she gasp? Scream? Weep? Laugh? Sit there in a daze?

Thanks to Scripture, we can at least be sure of what she *said*. With childlike simplicity, with honest words that only an innocent teen could say, Mary responded to the angel with a simple, direct question. A question that also sent shock waves across the galaxies.

"How will this be," she asked the angel, "since I am a virgin?"

In all of the universe, since space and time began, never had anything like this happened! God was about to become man. And this girl from Nazareth would never be the same.

As you read these words, ask yourself the same question as Mary: *How can this be?* It's a simple, direct question. An honest question. So ask yourself. And when you find the answer, *God became man for…you,* you also will never be the same.

A Plan behind the Pain

In those days Caesar Augustus issued a decree that a census should be taken of the entire Roman world…. And everyone went to his own town to register.

"So Joseph also went up from the town of Nazareth in Galilee to Judea, to Bethlehem the town of David, because he belonged to the house and line of David. He went there to register with Mary, who was pledged to be married to him and was expecting a child. While they were there, the time came for the baby to be born…" (Luke 2:1, 3–6).

The distance between Nazareth and Bethlehem is no Girl Scout hike. It spans over sixty miles of rough and rugged terrain.

We can imagine Joseph packing a few belongings and beginning that journey on foot or donkey-back with Mary—well into her ninth month of pregnancy. Talk about unpleasant circumstances! How Mary must have suffered on that journey. Joseph, too, may have been gripped by anxiety over the situation. Can you imagine his thoughts as they traveled toward Bethlehem?

Why did this census have to happen now? Of all times! What if the baby comes while we're traveling? Where will we stay when we get to Bethlehem? What if the inns are full? When the time comes, what if there is no one to help? Will I be able to assist Mary? Will it be terribly hard on her? Will the child be in danger?

But it was necessary to make that several-day journey to Bethlehem—for more reasons than one. Hundreds of years before, God prompted His prophet to name the town of the future Messiah's birth. The city of David. God used an external circumstance, the Roman census, to have His Son born in His ancestral city.

Now, certainly, it was a great inconvenience to both Mary and Joseph. But unpleasant circumstances often have a way of becoming the best part of God's magnificent design. Despite the headache and hardship, the inconvenience and discomfort, God's sovereign timetable was ticking off right on schedule.

This Christmas story has a lesson for us today, because sometimes you and I make the mistake of thinking that only the "right" things or comfortable things are a part of God's design. A good job, robust health, close friends, a comfortable house, money in a savings account—all give us the impression that we must be doing something "right." Then, when the inconvenience or discomfort or hardship hits, we wonder what "went wrong."

Maybe nothing went wrong.

Maybe we simply need to realize that our most unpleasant circumstances, much like Mary's and Joseph's, often have a way of becoming a beautiful portion of God's magnificent design.

God's sovereign timetable is working in the life of your family, too, hard as that may be to accept at times. Despite the hardship, despite the inconvenience, despite our lack of understanding, God has something in mind. He *is* in control, and He has a design for your life this Christmas season…and through all the seasons of your life.

THE STABLE

It was a chilly night in the little Judean town of Bethlehem. The kind of night when you want to escape the cold, damp air and find warmth and security inside a cozy inn. And people crowded tightly into the inn at the end of the street. They left their donkeys and camels in the back stable and closed the door against the night air.

Inside, the inn buzzed with laughter and chatter. Distant relatives who had not seen each other in years renewed family ties over bowls of hot soup and goblets of wine. They broke bread together, swapping stories of their journeys. A teenage boy strummed his lyre in the corner, and several fathers clapped their hands in time to the music.

In the rush to serve tables, the innkeeper, balancing a tray of breads and meats, answered a knock at the door. A man calling himself Joseph stood outside, pulling his homespun cloak tightly around his neck. It was late, it was cold, and he and his young wife needed a room. A glance told the innkeeper the woman was heavy with child. He could barely hear himself talk with so much noise behind him, but he managed to explain that there was no room, only an empty stall or two in the stable out back.

Shrugging his shoulders, the innkeeper quickly apologized and slammed the door. Outside, Joseph stood for a moment, listening to the laughter inside. Back in the stillness of the night, Mary waited. The young couple made their way to the stable. And while music

and laughter and feasting went on and on, just yards away behind the walls of the inn, the Son of God quietly entered history.

Sometimes the best moments of the Christmas season do not happen during the crowded parties or the rush of holiday preparations. They don't occur in the music and laughter, the camaraderie and feasting.

When I think of special Christmas memories, I think of those quiet moments when God unexpectedly surprised me. With Himself. With an overwhelming sense of His nearness and love.

In the midst of so much activity, so much going on, so many days on the calendar filled with appointments or parties, God seeks out the quiet heart…and speaks to us in a still, small voice.

Think of the stable in Bethlehem. Somehow it stands serene. What a contrast to the celebrating going on in that inn. Who would have supposed? Who would have suspected? If someone had only taken the time to peer out a back window toward the stable. If someone had only dropped what he was doing to leave the party and go check on his donkey. If someone had only slipped away from the festivities for a moment to seek a quiet moment outside.

Just think of what they might have witnessed! Perhaps they would have seen the angels. Maybe the shepherds. And, yes, even the Son of God.

Take time this Christmas season to step outside the clamor and excitement. Visit the stable and ask God to speak to you in the quiet and serenity and stillness.

He will.

SILENT NIGHT

"Silent night, holy night,
All is calm, all is bright
Round yon virgin mother and Child…"

What images do those words bring to your mind? Something warm and tender? Does the melody draw you into that darkened stable? Does it draw your eyes to the wondering eyes of a young virgin? Who was this Mary, who held the Savior of the world in her arms?

She was no prophetess of renown. She wasn't world famous. She probably wasn't even known beyond the small neighborhood where she grew up. Men and women didn't seek out her wisdom and advice. She was a simple young woman. A teenage girl. She wasn't a princess, and never enjoyed a fairy-tale life. The rich and influential paid her no heed. In their minds, it was as if she never even existed. She wasn't a brilliant scholar. She never had the benefit of sitting among the best teachers and philosophers of her day.

To be sure, Mary did have the blood of kings running in her veins. She was of the house of David and certainly was neither untaught nor unskilled. The song of praise which burst from her lips—the song generations have known as the Magnificat—tells us that she had a bright mind and a heart full of praise. But the point is, Mary, the young virgin chosen from thousands to be the mother of the Savior, was just a simple peasant girl. But oh, so available to God!

Even though her position was humble, God had chosen her above all the other women to be blessed in a very special way. Christ the King would be born to her, and *that* was an honor far beyond any title, certificate, or prominence in the social register.

Does that speak to you today? You may not have the benefit of a Bible college or seminary. You may not be very well known. You haven't shared your testimony in front of churches. There may not be many who even know your name. You're not particularly wealthy or wise. People don't knock on your door, seeking your advice or counsel. No titles, certificates, or honors distinguish you from the crowd. You're just…typical. With a normal job and a so-so standard of living. Nothing extraordinary.

But there is something extraordinary about Christ being born in your heart, isn't there? There is something special and unique about having Jesus live within you. And although you may not be wealthy or wise in the eyes of the world, the very riches of His kingdom have been promised to you. The Word of Christ can dwell in you richly, giving you His very mind. And if you remain available to Him, He will use you to accomplish His wise and mighty plans in this old world.

When you think about it, what worldly honors compare to those honors? What privileges stack up alongside those privileges?

Like Mary, you have something to sing about this Christmas season! Because God has chosen you. Because you've been blessed. Christ the King has been born—not just in a stable, but in your heart.

THE MAGNIFICAT

"My soul glorifies the Lord

and my spirit rejoices in God my Savior,

for he has been mindful of the humble state of his servant.

From now on all generations will call me blessed,

for the Mighty One has done great things for me—

holy is his name.

His mercy extends to those who fear him,

from generation to generation.

He has performed mighty deeds with his arm;

he has scattered those who are proud in their inmost thoughts.

He has brought down rulers from their thrones

but has lifted up the humble.

He has filled the hungry with good things

but has sent the rich away empty.

He has helped his servant Israel, remembering to be merciful

to Abraham and his descendants forever,

even as he said to our fathers."

LUKE 1:46–55

THE GREATEST MIRACLE

Have you ever wondered what might have been God's greatest miracle? There are certainly enough from which to choose.

Think of the Old Testament miracles like the destruction of Sodom and Gomorrah, the parting of the Red Sea, or the day the sun stood still in the heavens at the prayer of Joshua. Or how about creation itself? A universe leaping into existence at the merest word of the mighty Creator!

Over in the New Testament you could include Jesus turning water into wine, walking on water, quieting an angry sea, or raising the dead.

The list is long, the examples are many, and I'm sure the debate could go on indefinitely. But, let me propose a miracle in a class by itself…

Consider the fullness of God—the God who set suns and stars in motion, carved out rivers, puckered up mountain ranges, ladled out seas, dreamed up time and space, and formed you and me in the womb. Then imagine this same God coming to earth as an infant! God—the very essence of love and holiness, justice and mercy—this God entering history *in baby flesh*. The very voice which once spoke creation into being, now crying for mother's milk. The eyes of the Ancient of Days that roamed to and fro throughout the galaxies, now new, blurred, and teary. *God*…with little pink hands. Little nubby feet. Soft, silky hair and fresh, dewy skin.

What miracle can compare with that?

Shaking his head in wonder, the apostle writes of the One...

Who, being in very nature God,
did not consider equality with God something to be grasped,
but made himself nothing,
taking the very nature of a servant,
being made in human likeness.
And being found in appearance as a man,
he humbled himself....

PHILIPPIANS 2:6-8

I don't think there's any question. Those words describe the greatest miracle of all. When you think about it, the incarnation is such a mind-staggering miracle it makes the rest of those miracles seem almost secondary.

If we can believe that God came in the flesh, then all the other miracles are simple. Changing water into wine? Nothing to it. Opening blind eyes? Child's play! Raising men from the dead? No great matter for the Lord Jesus. The biggest miracle of all, the miracle of His birth, makes all the other stunning things that happened seem minor. Almost simple.

In this season of wonder and rejoicing over the greatest miracle of all, I join with you in adoration of our God who has come in the flesh. What a miracle!

Come, let us adore Him!

THE DAY AFTER

Here it is, the day after Christmas. You shove the boxes of unwrapped gifts to the side of the living room, picking up the leftover pieces of wrapping paper. Perhaps this morning you brew a pot of coffee and sit down to read yesterday's paper that got lost in the shuffle. The excitement has come down a notch or two, and things are edging back toward routine.

I wonder what the day after the first Christmas was like?

What happened the morning after that marvelous night when angels had burst out of the heavens and the Son of God was born? When the next day dawned was anything…different?

Picture it. The census was still going on in Bethlehem. Inside the crowded inn—the inn from which Mary and Joseph were turned away—the day began with a clamor. Families coming out of their rooms, heading downstairs for breakfast. Men stretching and yawning, women packing and preparing. Children pouring out of the inn into the streets to chase barking dogs and throw pebbles at chickens.

That morning the streets must have awakened early with the shift of Roman soldiers who were setting up the census tables.

"All right now, people. Everybody with a last name beginning with A to M head over there; the rest line up over here." That sort of thing.

I wonder if anyone bothered to mention the arrival of the young couple the night before. I wonder if the innkeeper, who was busy serving breakfast, ever stopped to ask one of his stable hands about the pregnant girl and her husband whom he had sent back to the barn. Did anyone ask how they were doing? I'm sure at least a few travelers headed for the stable to get their animals. Did any of them hear the cry of a newborn in the far stall as they untied their donkeys and loaded up?

Maybe yes, maybe no. Anyway, there were things to do and places to go. Just another ordinary day with ordinary demands. Wasn't much time to think about it.

No one could have begun to imagine what had happened the night before. Scant yards from where they slept, *God* entered the world as a baby.

Whether the heedless crowds realized it or not, no day could be called ordinary again. Forever.

SIMEON'S MESSAGE

Just imagine what must have gone through Mary's mind as she wrapped her newborn infant in a blanket and proceeded to Jerusalem to present Him to the Lord. That's what you did back then. Every firstborn male was to be consecrated to the Lord, and Mary and Joseph were obliged to go to the temple to present an offering for Him.

I can just picture the scene. Mary, with Baby Jesus in her arms, probably had a hard time getting through the groups of women in the temple courtyard.

"Oh my, is that your new baby? What's his name? Jesus? How nice. And so *cute!* Little hands, little fingers…hello there, little boy."

"Now, young woman," a few probably said as they turned to Mary, "you *are* going to be sure not to spoil him, aren't you?"

Mary must have blushed with so many well-wishers, everybody wanting to see a newborn baby, to "ooh and aah" over her infant boy. And she must have smiled extra big when all the old women told her how *special* her child looked. If only they knew!

At least two of those greetings were very unusual. One was frightening. It came from a stranger, an old man named Simeon who had an unusual fire burning in his eyes. He stopped Mary and asked if he might hold the child in his arms. Mary probably glanced at Joseph, got the nod, and gingerly placed her baby in the arms of this man (letting others hold her baby was getting to be a regular thing).

Just listen to what happened next:

Simeon took him in his arms and praised God, saying:

"Sovereign Lord, as you have promised,
you now dismiss your servant in peace.
For my eyes have seen your salvation,
which you have prepared in the sight of all people,
a light for revelation to the Gentiles
and for glory to your people Israel."

The child's father and mother marveled at what was said about him. Then Simeon blessed them and said to Mary, his mother: "This child is destined to cause the falling and rising of many in Israel, and to be a sign that will be spoken against, so that the thoughts of many hearts will be revealed. And a sword will pierce your own soul too."
(Luke 2:28–35)

How strange. It must have alarmed Mary when this odd old man spoke directly to her. Maybe it was something in his eyes…a seriousness, a sadness. But he spoke firmly and forthrightly. *"A sword will pierce your own soul."*

Hardly the thing you'd say to a new mother. Not what you'd call a polite greeting to give someone—that the tiny baby you're holding in your arms will be the cause of a deep and stabbing pain—like a sword thrust.

It was an ominous message, dark and foreboding. Even frightening. But perhaps it was God's way of reminding Mary—of reminding us—that the Son of God did not come just to bring peace, but to bring a sword.

Jesus Himself would echo the words of Simeon many years later. His own words sounded just as dark, just as ominous. And just as frightening. A Christmas message? Simeon would say so. Just listen to the words of his Lord and ours:

"I did not come to bring peace, but a sword…. Whoever finds his life will lose it, and whoever loses his life for my sake will find it." (Matthew 10:34, 39)

Chances are you won't see those verses woven into many Christmas wreaths this year. You won't see them stamped in silver on snow scenes when you open your Christmas cards. But the words are the words of Emmanuel, God-with-us. His coming turned the world upside down. Homes were divided, lives disrupted, blood shed. Nations rose and nations toppled because of His advent.

It's the same today. Lives hinge and eternal destinies hang in the balance when men and women come face to face with Jesus the Christ. It isn't always peaceful. It isn't always painless. It isn't always easy. But bowing the knee to Jesus Christ is always right. No matter what.

ANNA

I love little old ladies. Maybe it's because I'm growing older myself. Maybe it's because my own mother is in her eighties. I don't know what it is, but I love spending time talking to a woman who's been around awhile, a woman who's seen life with its ups and downs…and *especially* an older woman who loves the Lord Jesus.

I enjoy hearing anybody over the age of seventy-five sing "The Old Rugged Cross." I love to watch wrinkled hands hold a hymnbook. I love to see the smile come across an older woman's face when she sings "I come to the garden alone." Those hymns are never more beautiful than when they are sung by godly, saintly women…older women.

Maybe I would have felt that way about Anna. You remember her story. Anna, it says in Luke chapter 2, was a prophetess and very old—eighty-four in fact. Not only that, the Bible tells us she was a widow.

But this wasn't just *any* eighty-four-year-old widow. Scripture says that Anna never left the temple, but worshiped night and day, fasting and praying.

I wonder if people of her day and age looked askance at her. No doubt she was a bit…different. It sounds as though she virtually lived in the temple courtyard. Maybe some looked down on her as though she were the temple bag lady. Others surely saw her as a saint of the age.

When Mary and Joseph brought the baby Jesus into the temple to be consecrated, they had no idea what was about to happen. First, the strange and foreboding greeting of Simeon. With those words still hanging in the air, the Bible says that Anna came right up to them at that very moment, gave thanks to God, and spoke about the Child to everybody who was there. She even called Him "the redemption of Jerusalem."

I love to picture it! This saintly old woman wrapped her wrinkled hands around the infant Jesus and pronounced a beautiful blessing upon Him. Anna had the chance to celebrate the birthday of Jesus in the way it ought to be celebrated.

We can learn a thing or two from older women. And this Christmas we can learn how to celebrate the season from just looking at Anna. Let's pattern our celebration and worship after what she did in the temple that day. Christmas is a time for pronouncing beautiful blessings upon the Child of God. It's a time for giving heartfelt thanks to the Lord. It's a time to speak about the Christ-child to all who will listen. It's a time to talk about redemption.

Isn't it just like the Lord to let a humble older woman lead the way for all of us? Anna's pattern for Christmas celebration hasn't been improved upon in two thousand years.

MARY'S SONG

The figurative language of the poet opens doors in our thinking, expands our vision, and helps us dream the kind of dreams we never would have imagined ourselves.

Christmas is rich with the kind of substance that can be woven into beautiful imagery for us to ponder. I'm thinking of a favorite poem of mine, written by Luci Shaw. A poem entitled "Mary's Song"…

Blue homespun and the bend of my breast
keep warm this small hot naked star
fallen to my arms. (Rest…
you who have had so far
to come.) Now nearness satisfies
the body of God sweetly. Quiet he lies
whose vigor hurled
a universe. He sleeps
whose eyelids have not closed before.
His breath (so slight it seems
no breath at all) once ruffled the dark deeps
to sprout a world.

Charmed by dove's voices, the whisper of straw,
he dreams,
hearing no music from his other spheres.
Breath, mouth, ears, eyes,
he is curtailed
who overflowed all skies,
all years.
Older than eternity, now he
is new. Now native to earth as I am, nailed
to my poor planet, caught that I might be free,
blind in my womb to know my darkness ended,
brought to this birth
for me to be new-born,
and for him to see me mended
I must see him torn.[1]

What were her thoughts...as she cradled divinity in her lap? The wonder that must have filled her heart—and the pain—to know that one day her baby child would be torn.

This is the substance of Christmas. Something to ponder, something to consider. Something to draw threads of wonder from the most tired and cynical of hearts.

This Jesus, older than eternity, will make you new.

[1] Luci Shaw, "Mary's Song" in *Listen to the Green* (Wheaton, Ill.: Harold Shaw Publishers, 1971), 36. Used by permission.

Christmas Today . . .

WHAT OUR LONGINGS REVEAL

The people walking in darkness have seen a great light;
on those living in the land of the shadow of death a light has dawned.
You have enlarged the nation and increased their joy;
they rejoice before you as people rejoice at the harvest....
You have shattered the yoke that burdens them,
the bar across their shoulders, the rod of their oppressor.

ISAIAH 9:2–4

Sing to the LORD a new song,

for he has done marvelous things.

PSALM 98:1

"Merry Xmas" blinking in neon red. Dirty snow piled high in the gutter. Harried shoppers shoving in line. Huge savings if you open a Christmas credit account and purchase three pairs of anything.

If you look around, plenty of things during the holidays will break your heart. We feel the sting in our chest when we hear "Joy to the World" sung slurred and off-key at an office party. "This isn't right," we cry. "It's Christmas!"

We long to hallow the holidays. We want to create a celebration that's pure and pristine. But when we try to listen to the real song of Christmas, the noise and glitter drown it out. The song refuses to compete with greed and grime, and so it retires. We become our ordinary selves, shoveling dirty snow and shelving our childlike wonder over the Savior's birth. We sigh and consign our Christmas longings to some other time.

Don't let it happen. Your longings for a pure Christmas mustn't be put on the shelf. God has placed within your heart a nostalgia for Himself. He wants to be the center of your deepest desires this season. The perfect Christmas *is* possible when Christ is completely at its center.

So look around. Let a spray of snow touch your face and remind you of the way the Spirit of Christ moves. Listen to a music box play "Silent Night" and hear the still small voice of God. Gaze at a candle glowing in the night, and be reminded how His light shines in darkness.

Best of all, the next time you sing "Joy to the World," let His smile lift your voice.

A perfect Christmas...is a longing fulfilled.

CREATE YOUR
CHRISTMAS SPIRIT

It happens every year just about…now!

You hear a carol or two on the radio. You're startled by a sudden blaze of colored lights across the street. The mail carrier hands you a couple of square, red or green envelopes from another part of the country. Someone happens to mention that there are only twenty-five more shopping days until…

Yikes! You can't believe it. Christmas is about to happen, and you have no idea where the time has gone. Seems just yesterday you noticed that first hint of fall in the air and a tinge of gold in the leaves.

Now here you are, staring numbly at that last sheet on the calendar. You feel a growing pressure to somehow "get into the Christmas spirit." Out of nowhere, you feel wistful longings, a kind of funny nostalgia, a *need* to make this Christmas meaningful.

Now, you can do one of two things. You can simply wait around for the Christmas spirit to hit you (it may or may not), or you can *create* the spirit.

How, you may ask, do you accomplish that? Believe it or not, it's really quite simple. And even though December may have barely arrived, there's good reason to begin planning a very memorable and meaningful Christmas.

The most important step is the way you get started. You can begin by adoring, worshiping, thinking, and meditating on all that the birth of the Lord Jesus means to you. And *now* is the best time to do it.

Maybe that's why God puts those wistful longings in our hearts this time of year. He wants us to find the answer to those longings in the celebration of Jesus. He wants us to define that nostalgia as nothing more than a deep human desire to come home and adore His Son.

To be sure, holly and ivy, cider and pine trees help those sentimental feelings, those poignant, dreamy longings for the "perfect Christmas." Those things are nice. But there's nothing like creating the real Christmas spirit by worshiping and adoring Jesus.

Okay, so it's still early. So the lights are still going up around the neighborhood. Don't you dare let the Christmas crunch pressure you in these days ahead! Don't get lost in the whirlwind of jingles and commercials and holiday sales. And please, please, don't let the frazzle of these next few weeks rob you of the real joy of this time of year.

Get a head start with the right perspective. Now's the time to put it all in focus. Create your own Christmas spirit—that wonderful spirit of gratitude and thanksgiving for God's greatest Gift, that genuine spirit of Christmas, the birth of the Lord Jesus. That Gift will meet every longing, every nostalgic, wistful need this season brings to mind.

Yes, you may still be getting used to the idea that November is history and December is on your doorstep. But *anytime* of *any* month is the best time to celebrate Jesus.

THE CHRISTMAS PAGEANT

This is the month when schools and churches all over the country are holding their annual Christmas pageants. Probably the best Christmas pageant story I ever heard was the one about Wally Purling, printed in *Guideposts* magazine years ago.

As the story goes, Wally was nine that year and in second grade—although he should have been in fourth. Most folks in town knew he had difficulty keeping up. He was big and clumsy, slow in movement and mind. Still, Wally was well liked by the other children in his class, all of whom were smaller than he. He was always helpful, the natural protector of the underdog.

Wally fancied the idea of being a shepherd with a flute in the Christmas pageant that year. But the director of the play, Miss Lumbard, assigned him to a "more important" role. After all, she reasoned, the innkeeper didn't have too many lines.

So it happened that the usual large audience gathered for the town's yearly extravaganza of crowns and halos, shepherds' crooks and beards, and a whole stage full of squeaking voices. But no one on stage or off was more caught up in the magic of the night than Wally Purling.

The time came when Joseph appeared, slowly, tenderly guiding Mary to the door of the inn. Joseph knocked hard on the wooden door of the painted backdrop.

"What do you want?" Wally said, swinging the door open.

"We seek lodging."

"Seek it elsewhere." Wally looked straight ahead and spoke vigorously. "The inn is full."

"Sir, we have asked everywhere in vain. We have traveled far and are very weary."

Wally looked stern. "There is no room in this inn for you."

Joseph put his arm around Mary. "Please, good innkeeper, this is my wife, and she is heavy with child and needs a place to rest. Surely you must have some small corner for her."

For the first time, Wally the innkeeper relaxed his stiff stance and looked down at Mary. There was a long pause—long enough to make the audience a bit tense with embarrassment. A prompter whispered from the wings, "Your line is 'No! Be gone!' "

Wally repeated automatically, "Be gone!"

Joseph sadly placed his arm around Mary, and the two of them started moving away. Wally stood there in the doorway, watching. Suddenly his eyes filled with tears. And suddenly this Christmas pageant became different from all others.

"Wait!" Wally the innkeeper suddenly blurted out. "Don't go, Joseph." His face broke into a wide smile. "You can have *my* room."

Many people in town thought the program had been ruined. A few, however—the thoughtful ones—considered it the most meaningful pageant of all.

In from the Cold

As a kid, I loved staying outside in the cold winter snow as long as I could. I'd look like the Michelin tire guy, I'd be so bundled up. I'd plop myself in a big white drift and sit there rather amazed that I could see my frosty breath and yet feel so toasty warm. That didn't last long, though. I'd play until my fingers got cold and numb. But did I have sense enough to go inside?

Of course not! I don't know what it is about kids, but they will nearly freeze their tails off and still refuse to come inside the house until they're called. I actually remember thinking, *Man, my feet are like icicles. I wish Mom would call me inside.* But would I go inside of my own accord? Not a chance.

Yet when Mom finally would call, oh, it felt so good to swing open the back door and step across the threshold into a warm house!

There's a special feeling you get when you walk inside a warm, inviting home. It's a sense of belonging, a sense that you're welcome, that you're wanted. And the cold air outside only makes you feel all the better about being inside!

But why, tell me why, do so many of us *insist* on staying outside in the cold? You hear stories of how lonely the Christmas season is for many people. You may even count yourself one of them. You long to be a part of the fellowship, the friendship, but you find yourself waiting…waiting for someone to call you inside, hoping that someone will invite you in. The Christmas carols only make you feel nostalgic for a home you don't have. Christmas cards only make you feel guilty that you haven't taken time to write and send them yourself.

I don't mean to sound cruel, but it's almost as though you *want* to stay on the outside of the Christmas cheer. And if nobody throws open the front door to welcome you into their joy, you stubbornly think to yourself, "Well, that's me, just one of the holiday statistics of lonely people."

You know what? You don't have to wait for someone to call you inside to get warm. *You* be the one who calls. *You* be that someone to reach out to another. *You* welcome someone in and invite him or her to share the season with you. This is what Jesus would do, and this is what He wants for each one of us. There's simply no reason to stay outside in the lonely wind, stubbornly waiting for someone else to "make our Christmas special."

The Lord Jesus wants you to invite another in. That's the best way to beat the loneliness. It's the best way to come in out of the cold.

O Little Town of Bethlehem

Who of us hasn't gone Christmas caroling at one time or another? Maybe it was to a nursing home or nearby hospital. Maybe you bundled up and huddled outside some neighbor's house, clutching a candle and making a joyful noise. Perhaps you invited some friends over for hot cider, pumpkin pie, and Christmas hymns sung around the piano.

Looking back on my childhood, I have rather unusual memories of Christmas caroling with my family. The Earecksons did it on *horseback*.

I couldn't have been more than five years old when I joined the family tradition, up on top of that big, old horse of mine. We galloped to a nearby farmhouse, pulled our horses up outside the neighbor's front door, got out hymnals from our saddlebags, and sang those beautiful choruses. You can imagine it gets pretty cold on those dark winter nights. That's when my father would pull out hot water bottles from his saddlebags and put them between us and the cold seat of our saddles. What a way to warm up!

More than just the memory of nighttime horseback rides through the snow, the most wonderful part for me was those beautiful Christmas carols. My favorite way back then was "O Little Town of Bethlehem." I especially loved the verse that says, "O little town of

Bethlehem, how still we see thee lie! Above thy deep and dreamless sleep the silent stars go by...." Even though I was just a child, the words of that carol painted a wondrous picture in my mind of what that starry night must have been like.

The days of horseback caroling seem long ago and faraway now. Even so, "O Little Town of Bethlehem" still stirs me deeply. But these days I cling to lines in that carol which hold a far deeper meaning for me. The last verse reads: "O Holy Child of Bethlehem, descend to us we pray; Cast out our sin and enter in; be born in us today."

Serious words for a Christmas carol, don't you think? Jesus isn't simply a baby adored in some distant and ancient manger. He isn't simply a convenient centerpiece for holiday parties and family gatherings.

Christ had a purpose in coming. And Christmas has meaning because of these words: "Cast out our sin and enter in; be born in us today."

When I was a child, even though the Christmas memories were very precious to me, I'm not so sure I caught the full meaning behind the birth of Christ.

But I do now. And I trust that in the midst of this sometimes frantic time of year, you too will understand. May the Christ we worship enter your heart today, casting out any sin that stands in the way. And if you don't already know Him, may He be born in you... right now.

IN A QUIET PLACE

The clouds were low and gray, like the down of goose feathers. As the snow fell in light, dry flakes, a gray-white haze made our barn and springhouse almost disappear.

I leaned on my elbow looking out the window while my mom and sisters busied themselves in the kitchen, cooking the food and setting the table for Christmas Eve dinner. An aunt and uncle were visiting, along with a few cousins, a neighbor, and several friends. The house was busy with a pleasant bustling about. Christmas carols from the kitchen radio drifted into the living room where I sat on the window seat staring outside. I was a child, with no particular responsibilities for the preparations.

Sometime during the late afternoon, while the sky grayed further, I pulled on my jacket and boots, stuffed a few carrots and apples in my pockets, and hiked to the stable. I felt sorry for the horses and goats in the barn. All of us were going to open Christmas presents that evening, and I didn't want the animals to be left out.

It was quiet in the stable. I recall the sweet smell of hay, the cozy odors of the horses' coats. Someone had fed them that morning, but I opened the feed bin and gave each horse an extra handful of oats along with a carrot or an apple.

Something about the peace and quiet of that stable warmed me through and through…as warm as though I were sitting by the fire back up at the farmhouse. Maybe it was because I was alone. Maybe it was because I took time to think while watching the

horses crunch their gifts. Maybe it was the beauty of solitude contrasted against the bustling cheer inside the house. But in some way God spoke to me that afternoon. Even as a little girl, I knew I was making a Christmas memory which would last forever.

Maybe you don't live on a farm. Perhaps when you look outside your window, you see the backyard of your next-door neighbor. Or you may live in an apartment. Or a trailer. Maybe there are palm trees outside your kitchen door. Or sagebrush. You could be in a hospital. Or prison. Or a nursing home.

Not many of us live near a stable. But you know what I'm talking about. Find that place to be apart. A place of quiet and solitude. It could be a window seat and a cup of Café Français. It could be a walk through a nearby park with a Bible in hand. It could be the cool quiet of an upstairs bedroom. Wherever it is, make sure you're alone. With Him.

You can be sure the Christmas memory you create with God and His Word will last a lifetime.

"Be still, and know that I am God;
I will be exalted among the nations,
I will be exalted in the earth."

The LORD Almighty is with us;
the God of Jacob is our fortress.

PSALM 46:10-11

CELEBRATE SIMPLICITY

Let us fix our eyes on Jesus" is a verse to keep in mind all year long. You know as well as I do that fixing your eyes on Jesus can drastically alter your lifestyle. Your values. Your home budget. Your taste in fashions. The way you converse with your neighbor. How you spend your time.

It all boils down to simplicity. A lifestyle, a budget, a wardrobe, an appointment calendar which reflect simplicity.

So why is it that during the Christmas season—the season when more than ever we are to have our eyes fixed on Jesus—that simplicity goes out the window? Simplicity gets buried under the load of shopping bags on the dining-room table. Simplicity gets lost among the crowd of appointments and parties that fill our holiday schedule. And as far as a budget is concerned, simplicity is forgotten as we spend far beyond our means on gifts or a holiday wardrobe.

Just what is it about Christmas that makes us go overboard?

We say we fix our eyes on Jesus, yet in the same breath we overextend, overcommit, and overwhelm ourselves as December 25 draws near.

It's funny, but one of my favorite days in the entire holiday season is December 26. Maybe it's because there's a sigh of relief. The harried expressions, rushed conversations, and frantic last-minute purchases are gone. We sit around and munch leftovers. We have more time to lounge on the couch in front of the fire and play board games or reopen gifts to take a closer, longer look. We nibble day-old pie and keep warm a pot of tea for anyone who may happen to drop by. It's casual. It's home. It's relaxed. But most important, it's simple.

So this year, let's aim for deliberate simplicity. What are some of your easiest and favorite recipes? Why not cook those, rather than going all out for a family gathering? Resist the temptation to do everything "different" this year. It doesn't have to be bigger or more expensive. Give thoughtful love gifts, maybe limiting yourself, but better yet, sticking to a budget. Dress up your holiday wardrobe from last year with nice, inexpensive accessories. I know my mom enjoys picking out a small Christmas ornament ahead of time and pinning it on her red sweater.

Instead of Mom and Dad heading out to a party and leaving the kids behind, purpose to plan more family activities. Go to a church concert and sit together in one pew rather than one person heading off to sit with the junior highers or another sitting with the college-career group.

Bake, frost, and wrap cookies together as a family. Make certain to decorate the tree together as a family. Play a couple of board games, and have one of your children be responsible for choosing or serving dessert.

As at no other time during the entire year, we need to fix our eyes on Jesus. Don't let a simple encouragement like that get buried, lost, or forgotten.

Keep it simple. Keep your eyes on Him.

Shout for joy to the LORD, all the earth,

burst into jubilant song with music;

make music to the LORD with the harp,

with the harp and the sound of singing,

with trumpets and the blast of the ram's horn—

shout for joy before the LORD, the King.

Let the sea resound, and everything in it,

the world, and all who live in it.

Let the rivers clap their hands,

let the mountains sing together for joy;

let them sing before the LORD.

PSALM 98:4-9

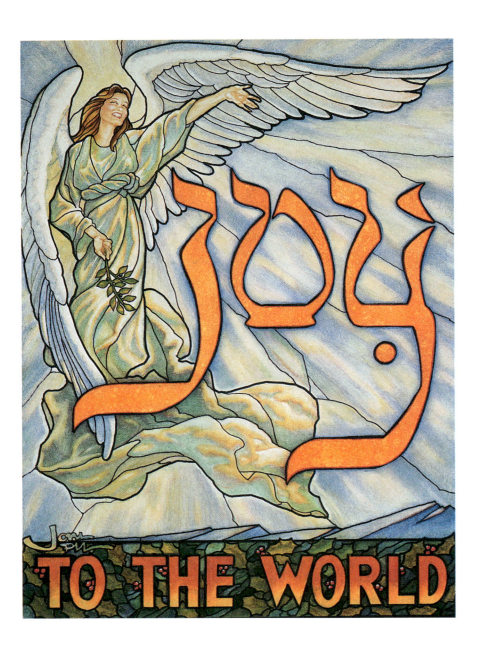

It's Christmas! Rejoice!

One minute the skies over Bethlehem were cool and quiet; the next minute someone turned on a light switch. Stars that were twinkling suddenly blazed in heavenly glory, and an angel stepped out of the divine fireworks to announce to shepherds on the hillside, "I bring you good news of great joy that will be for all the people."

Artists have tried for ages to capture that moment on canvas. How do you paint an angel…much less one rejoicing? I sat in front of my easel for a long time pondering that one. All I came up with were musty images of demure and dispassionate beings clasping their hands, looking heavenward and whispering in thick Oxford accents, "Rejoice." That just didn't sit right.

We're talking joy here. Jump up and down, dance, throw your head back and yell out loud, "Rejoice!" Kick your heels together and shout hallelujah! A Savior has come!

Sound a little…irreligious?

Maybe to some, but not to God. When God talks about joy, it doesn't mean plaster-of-Paris saints uttering amazement in less-than-amazing tones. In Luke chapter 6 Jesus says, "Rejoice in that day and leap for joy, because great is your reward in heaven." That's no sedate and dispassionate command. You can't be dignified and demure when you're exclaiming.

Jesus was telling His friends to leap for joy. I've heard scholars interpret that with upraised arms and clenched fists, yelling, "Oh, joy!" There's power-packed emotion in the Lord's words.

And when the angel announced good tidings, I reasoned while sitting in my art studio, *I believe that angel was bursting with joy. After all, it was the word of God, alive and active, full of feeling and brimming with heartfelt excitement.*

That's all the inspiration I needed. I reached for the pastel pencils with my mouth and began sketching what my mind saw, or rather, what my heart felt. Right away I realized I needed someone to model as an angel, so I called my secretary into the art studio and asked her to stand on a chair and drape a sheet around her.

"Now," I said when she was ready, "throw your arms out and yell, 'Surprise!' "

"What?" she asked with a funny look.

"Just think of your happiest memory, something that surprised your socks off and really made you smile."

She rubbed her chin until an idea dawned. Then throwing her head back, she hollered, "Whoopee!" I scribbled fast and even had a friend come in to snap a couple of pictures.

As I painted during the next few weeks, I pictured the Lord of joy and His smile. I got excited about the Good News. I imagined Mary beaming with pride and Joseph grinning. Even I, the artist, got into the spirit, laughing and throwing paint around on the canvas. The result? A truly happy angel sharing a message of…joy!

This month you'll see lots of Christmas cards and store windows displaying the word "Rejoice!" You'll sing about joy in carols and read about it in the pages of Scripture. Smile when you say it…or see it…or sing it.

Jesus is what the joy is all about.

GIVE YOURSELF

Does Christmas get you excited?

I love every minute of it. The tang of hot apple cider, the aroma of fresh pies in the oven, the carols by candlelight, and the worship and adoration of Jesus. Ken and I are going back East to visit my family on the farm, so the holidays will be complete with winter jackets and fresh falling snow. I'm hoping Ken will try his turn at horseback riding in the snow. I'm betting my brother-in-law will take him hunting down on the eastern shore or maybe up to the western Maryland mountains.

All this is going to be very new and exciting to my husband, who was born and raised in Burbank, California.

I'm sure we'll fellowship at Christmas Eve services as always and then return home for presents and singing. I've got great gift ideas this year, and I've been buying for months in advance to surprise my family with some very special gifts. All of us will no doubt be thinking of just the right gift for each other—something personal, something unusual, something "just right."

But as I make a mental list of all those gifts, I can't think of anything better to give than myself. My time, my interest, my love and appreciation for my mom or dad or sisters or in-laws. Nicely wrapped packages, gorgeous gifts, ornate cards—they can never take the place of the time, effort, or energy that you invest in your relationships with family and friends.

One young friend of mine thought of some very clever gift ideas that really were an investment of his time and energy. He gave the gift of himself...a month of Sundays to help his mom with dishes, five backrubs whenever his brother might ask, or the promise to stack the firewood and pile it high at the back door.

You and I should be the best gift that we could ever give to another. What about your gift list this Christmas? Nothing could say more than the time, interest, and love that you give a friend or loved one.

That's what God gave us when He gave Himself in the person of Jesus Christ. "God so loved the world that *He* gave"—and that's a theme meant to be repeated in the life of every believer this holiday season. So give yourself—your love.

It's the most valuable gift by far.

CHRISTMAS DECORATIONS

I wish you could see our Christmas tree this year.

Ken and I spent a little extra money to bring home the fullest, fattest, bushiest tree we could find on a southern California tree lot. Now its piney, outdoorsy fragrance fills our living room. I can close my eyes and catch a whiff of the high Sierras.

Like most families across the country, we unearthed our box of Christmas ornaments from the garage, carefully unwrapping each silver ball, each decoration we had collected over the years.

There's a little wooden horse I brought out from the farm years ago. It's hanging in its usual place near the top of the tree. There are little clothespin angels, soldiers, shepherds, and Santa Clauses a dear friend gave me when I moved to California. There's a shiny little silver ornament from Earecka. A polar bear made out of bread dough. A little cornhusk doll. A porcelain bell from my sister.

Each ornament is treasured. Each has its honored place on our tree. Each kindles a warm memory. Oh, to be sure, we've added silver icicles to our tree this year...sparkling wisps of cellophane that add excitement and catch the color of the lights, shimmering and shining even in the darkness.

But you know what? None of that sparkling stuff has any real meaning. When Ken and I untrim our tree in a week or two, the silver icicles will be dumped unceremoniously into the wastebasket.

But the ornaments? Ahh, they'll be treated with special care. Gently wrapped. Tenderly stored for another tree, another year, another Christmas. The things that have meaning will last like a rich treasure. Those things which hold no meaning—even though glittery and shimmery and eye-catching—will be forgotten.

It's kind of like that in life, isn't it? There are many dimensions to our lives—some last, and others, while they add sparkle, quickly fade.

What are the lasting things in your life this Christmas?

How about in the life of your family? Are you carefully accumulating treasured memories which are like old but lovely family ornaments you enjoy each Christmas season?

Is your first love for the Babe in the manger lasting in your heart over the years?

How about your desire for God's Word? Is it lasting over the frantic rush of the holidays?

I hope when you take away all the temporary glitter, you will find real love in your heart and in your home…love for God, love for family, love for others…love that endures.

Isn't that what Christmas is all about?

LUTHER'S CHRISTMAS TREE

Christmas trees are under attack by many good Christians these days. I've read some of the articles and listened to a few of the tapes explaining how Christmas trees and their decorations are throwbacks from pagan times…days when pagans celebrated their high winter holidays and used trees and decorations in their godless festivals.

I'm not going to argue. There's probably truth in what those people say. But frankly, I prefer the other rendition. The one about Martin Luther's experience with evergreen trees.

On a clear Christmas Eve night, Luther was walking home through the forest. Beyond the crisp, fragrant branches of the evergreens, he could see the twinkle of a thousand stars. The branches appeared to Luther as though they were wearing stars on their fingers. It must have been a beautiful sight. And on this special night, it was an experience of God's splendor that he wanted to share with his family.

He cut a small fir tree and carried it back to his home. As his children watched in wonder, Martin Luther lighted candles as stars and placed them on the little tree's branches. They must have stood together that night around the little tree and sung hymns of wonder to their Lord.

Though we do not know if this was really the first Christmas tree, down through the ages Christians have carried on this tradition. For many, the evergreen tree—in Latin, the *lignum vitae* or "tree of life"—represents wonderful truths from Scripture. Its green and lively branches are a vivid symbol of resurrection during a cold and barren season.

That's what I choose to think of when I sit back and enjoy the beautiful Christmas tree Ken and I have standing in the corner of our living room. It's not cluttered with a lot of unnecessary stuff so that you can't see the branches. Just a spray of tiny lights, a few family ornaments, and a star at the top. I like to think our simple little tree is very much like the one Papa Luther erected in his home that Christmas Eve so many years ago.

Listen, I don't like the idea of pagans taking something as beautiful as an evergreen tree (which, incidentally, God created for our pleasure…the devil didn't have anything to do with creating trees) and using it in some godless ceremony any more than the next person. But as Christians, we can ascribe beautiful and positive meaning to whatever God has created for our enjoyment.

I believe 1 Chronicles 16:33 is an apt description of our evergreen tree. It says there, "Then shall the trees of the wood sing out at the presence of the LORD" (KJV).

Somehow I think Martin Luther would have agreed.

Longing for...

HIS SECOND

ADVENT

For to us a child is born, to us a son is given,
and the government will be on his shoulders.
And he will be called Wonderful Counselor, Mighty God,
Everlasting Father, Prince of Peace.
Of the increase of his government and peace there will be no end.
He will reign on David's throne and over his kingdom, establishing and upholding it
with justice and righteousness from that time on and forever.

ISAIAH 9:6–7

The Spirit and the bride say, "Come!"

And let him who hears say, "Come!"

Whoever is thirsty, let him come;

and whoever wishes, let him take the free gift of the water of life. . . .

He who testifies to these things says,

"Yes, I am coming soon."

Amen. Come, Lord Jesus.

REVELATION 22:17, 20

Merry Christmas...
Happy holidays...
Season's greetings...
May the joy of the season be yours...

These are sweet words, simple greetings. Each phrase has a warm, candlelit glow to it, reminding me of the birth of Jesus so far away and long ago. But I have to admit, it's curious we've become so attached, almost affixed to these familiar words. We repeat them on nearly every card, see them painted on every store window, read them on countless church bulletins, and even jot them at the close of every personal letter we write during the holidays. It's as though each phrase takes us back in thought to that age-old, ever-wondrous night in history.

But "Merry Christmas" doesn't have to be always and only a harking back to the past. Yes, He *has* come, but the celebration need not remain in the past tense.

There's more, so much more.

"Merry Christmas" is only half the picture. Only part of the promise. An unfinished sentence. Christmas introduced us to the story of Advent, but there is a conclusion yet to be written. And what's the first word in that concluding drama?

Maranatha! Or as we say in modern English, "Come, Lord!"

Now *there's* a perfect Christmas greeting. Especially when we realize that Jesus is the answer to our deepest longings. Even Christmas longings. Each Advent brings us closer to His glorious return to earth. When we see Him as He is, King of kings and Lord of lords, that will be "Christmas" indeed!

Talk about giving Christmas gifts! Just think of this abundance…

You do not lack any spiritual gift as you eagerly wait for our Lord Jesus Christ to be revealed. (1 Corinthians 1:7)

And carols? You're about to hear singing like you've never heard before. Listen…

And I heard, as it were, the voice of a great multitude and as the sound of many waters and as the sound of mighty peals of thunder, saying, "Hallelujah! For the Lord our God, the Almighty reigns." (Revelation 19:6, NASB)

Christmas choirs? Never was there a choir like the one about to be assembled…

They held harps given them by God and sang…the song of the Lamb:

"Great and marvelous are your deeds, Lord God Almighty.

Just and true are your ways, King of the ages."

REVELATION 15:2–3

True, Main Street in your town may be beautifully decorated for the season, but picture this…

The twelve gates [of the city] were twelve pearls, each gate made of a single pearl. The great street of the city was of pure gold, like transparent glass. (Revelation 21:21)

Oh, and yes, we love the glow of candles on a cold winter's night and the twinkling of Christmas lights in the dark, but can you imagine this?

There will be no more night. They will not need the light of a lamp or the light of the sun, for the Lord God will give them light. And they will reign for ever and ever. (Revelation 22:5)

It's just around the corner, just over the rise. The leaves scattered over the end times are rustling with the rumor that His coming is near. Heaven is about to happen. The celebration is about to burst on the scene. We stand tiptoe at the edge of eternity, ready to step into the new heaven and new earth. And I can hardly wait.

Maranatha! Come, Lord! If I could, I would even now step into the other side of Christmas to see the promise fulfilled. I desire with all my heart to have my longings finally satisfied!

I can't wait to sing "O come, all ye faithful" as I gather with my friends and family to worship the Lord in heaven. I can't wait to give Him the gift of my refined faith, the "riches of his glorious inheritance in the saints." On bended knee, alongside kings and shepherds, together we will praise Him and sing "Glory to God in the highest!" And for eternity we will follow the One who is "the bright Morning Star" (Revelation 22:16).

Ahh, what glorious thoughts to comfort and encourage us as we look up into the frosty blanket of a million stars on these cold winter nights. If you've got a Christmas longing, you're about to be satisfied, too. Just hold on and say with me…*Maranatha!*

O Come, Emmanuel

One of the nicest things about being back East for Christmas is attending a few of those winter concerts around town. I remember one concert in an old Methodist church downtown. Outside it was cold, and a knifing wind made everybody pull their jackets and scarves tightly around them. But inside the old stone church, people left their coats and galoshes in the entry hall and huddled cozily in the dimly lit pews.

Candlelight bathed the sanctuary with a warm and inviting glow, and the voices of the choir echoed off the high church ceiling.

The memory of that beautiful, solemn time is as clear and crisp as the air of that winter night. I remember the choir singing,

> *O come, O come, Emmanuel,*
> *And ransom captive Israel,*
> *That mourns in lonely exile here*
> *Until the Son of God appear…*

There is something bittersweet, almost wistful, about that hymn. Even the tune is written in a minor key, a sad sort of piece to listen to at a Christmas concert…especially when you hear the melody echo in a lonely kind of way as it did that night in the old stone church.

One verse of that song reads:

O come, thou Dayspring, come and cheer
Our spirits by Thine advent here.
Disperse the gloomy clouds of night,
And death's dark shadows put to flight.

There's a kind of longing in those words, isn't there? They are words that could come right out of the depths of your heart when you feel captive by doubt or despair. Maybe you feel your own life could be sung in a minor key just now…saddened by a recent loss in the family or a trial that only piles your problems higher and higher, pressing your spirit down.

The text of that carol reflects such a mood. But there is more to that song! The words go on to include a triumphant chorus which echoes, "Rejoice, rejoice, Emmanuel shall come to thee, O Israel."

That's the hope that Christmas gives. Even though we may feel fogged in by those gloomy clouds of night, we have reason to rejoice. Yes, even in the middle of Christmas glitter and tinsel, our hearts may be in pain for one reason or another. And that's a bitter feeling, but also a sweet one. It's sweet because we have the promise that Emmanuel—"God with us"—shall come to us.

In other words, God will meet us where we are during these sometimes-dark December days. Christ has come for our redemption, and we have every reason to break forth with the resounding words, "Rejoice…rejoice…"

Long ago and far away in that old stone Methodist church, I rejoiced to sing that chorus of His coming. Thank the Lord, I'm still rejoicing to this day!

THE PROMISE

How long does it take for a dream to come true? How long does it take for a wish to be granted? When do you stop believing that a promise will ever be fulfilled?

Think about it. How long will you wait for a promise to be met before you stop believing? Weeks? Months? Maybe years?

Well, try centuries! If you take time to casually leaf through the pages of the Old Testament and into the New, you'll find that people hung onto the promise of God for a long, long time.

God announced His intentions about the Messiah when He made a promise to Abraham. And what did Abraham do? Romans 4:3 tells us that he believed God. That's all he needed to do. The rest was credited to him as righteousness.

But I wonder how Abraham felt two weeks later. Or months later. How did his children feel many years later? And what about his descendants, thousands of years later? How long did these people wait before they finally stopped believing?

The fact is, many did stop believing. They had no faith. They didn't reckon that God was a promise-keeper. As a result, they had no righteousness to their credit.

But others continued to believe. They dreamed of the day, they hoped for the future, they put their confidence in the promise of God. These, no doubt, were the ones who recognized Christmas when it happened. These were the ones who knew Jesus. These were those who waited for the promise. Even Zechariah in Luke chapter 1 said, "Praise be to the Lord, the God of Israel, because he has come…(as he said through his holy prophets of long ago)…to remember his holy covenant, the oath he swore to our father Abraham" (vv. 68, 70, 72–73).

Zechariah, and many like him, didn't stop believing. And their faith was credited to them as righteousness.

Maybe, just maybe, that's why you and I feel such…such nostalgic longings this time of year. True, the promised Messiah has come, but there's more, so much more to the promise. We will always experience a certain amount of unfulfilled longing until that day when Christ Himself comes back, as He promised, to live among us in unveiled majesty and splendor. Then, at last, there will be no more wistful longings, no need for nostalgia. We will know complete, unmixed joy.

Do you have those longings this season? If you do, then I'll just bet you're waiting for the promise to be fulfilled.

You're a believer. Across the many years, the many centuries, you're waiting with the rest of us for His promised return.

Never stop believing. Never stop hoping. Keep looking to the future. Keep half an eye on the clouds where He will appear to call us home.

God has promised. Let's believe it.

O Come, All Ye Faithful

Funny how little incidents from childhood seem to linger in the memory from year to year. Christmas sounds and sights and smells unlock a number of such memories.

When I hear the carol "O Come, All Ye Faithful," I think of a certain music box at my grandmother's.

Built of cream-colored plastic, it was shaped like a Gothic church, complete with all the arches, gables, and a big steeple with a cross on the top. As a child, I thought the windows were made of real stained glass. Every time Grandmother plugged it in, a light inside made those windows glow with a kaleidoscope of colors. Then she would wind it up, and the music box would play "O Come, All Ye Faithful."

I didn't know all the words to that song, but for minutes on end I would lay my head against my folded arms on the table and stare at that little glowing church. Mesmerized, I'd hum along with the tune.

Years later, that hymn is still a Christmas favorite.

"O come, all ye faithful, joyful and triumphant…"

I'm so glad I'm among "the faithful." Those words of the hymnist include me… and perhaps you who read these words. Who, after all, was the writer addressing with his invitation "Come, all ye faithful"?

Who are "the faithful"?

Well, there are those who are faithful in prayer. Faithful in good works. Faithful to commitments and vows made to spouses, families, and friends. Faithful in the face of crushing disappointments. Faithful to correct or admonish a friend, bringing him back to the path of right and light.

Faithfulness implies not only trust in Christ as Savior, but obedience to Him as Lord. Peter speaks of those who are "firm in the faith," resisting Satan though he prowls like a roaring lion (1 Peter 5:8–9). In Revelation 2:10, the risen Lord Jesus urges those facing bitter persecution to "be faithful, even to the point of death."

That same Lord, on the day when He welcomes us into heaven, will reward us with the words, "Well done, good and faithful servant."

Faithful means hanging in there.

Faithful means persevering and keeping on keeping on until that special day.

Faithful means believing what you've always believed and believing it all the more as the days go by.

Faithful means you don't quit, no matter what.

So come, all you faithful. You are the ones who are truly joyful and triumphant this Christmas season. And you are the ones called to come and adore Him, Christ our wonderful *and faithful* Lord.

PEACE ON EARTH

Peace on earth, good will toward men."

We read that phrase on Christmas cards. We hear it sung. We hear it from pulpits. Yet it's good to remember that the peace of which the angels sang that holy night had nothing to do with warm, fuzzy feelings.

They were announcing an end to a terrible war. A war between God and man.

During the Franco-Prussian War in 1870, French and German soldiers faced each other in opposite trenches on Christmas Eve.

While a light snow filled the sky and covered the ground in delicate white, a young Frenchman leaped out of his trench and began singing a beautiful French Christmas carol, "O Holy Night."

No one fired a shot. The Germans were awestruck, laying aside their weapons in momentary disbelief. Then a young German soldier climbed out of his trench and sang Martin Luther's Christmas hymn "From Heaven Above to Earth I Come."

After the soldier finished his solo, he returned to his trench. For the rest of that day, a calm and gentle peace fell over the battlefield…as calm and gentle as the flakes of snow which lightly touched the ground.

The bloody Franco-Prussian War for just a day…for just a moment…had stopped. The fighting was suspended. A truce, of sorts, was called.

For that moment, the heralding of another peace treaty rang across those camps. For the war between heaven and earth, God and man, ended with the birth, death, and resurrection of Jesus Christ. And the beautiful thing was this: it wasn't just for a day. The war had not simply been suspended. It wasn't a temporary truce.

You see, when Christ entered history, He didn't come waving a white flag. His coming was not simply a lull in the battle. It was more than a momentary cease-fire.

When the angels sang, "Peace on earth, good will toward men," they were announcing an armistice. It was V-Day. An end, not just to the battle between God and man, but to the war.

The phrase "peace on earth" carries with it so much more meaning than simply a warm, fuzzy feeling between the Lord and us.

Christ, our Prince of Peace, was God's way of announcing the close to an awful war. The Lord Jesus invaded enemy territory to lay claim on what was rightfully His. He confronted sin, and His battle cry told men that He had come to set them free. Through His death and resurrection, He signed the peace treaty with His own blood.

During this season we celebrate an end to the warfare. I'm so happy that Christmas is more than just a truce or a lull in the battle. The Lord Jesus Christ is our peace.

We have great reason to celebrate.

OUTSIDE IN

Christmas *has* to be something you share. The holiday just doesn't make much sense solo.

Can you imagine baking cookies, sprinkling little candies on them, arranging them nicely on a silver tray, and then…gulping them all down yourself? Great fun, huh?

What enjoyment would there be in decorating a tree all by yourself? You string the popcorn, get out the tinsel, hang the ornaments on the limbs, plug in the lights, and then…sit there alone?

Listen, if you're going to go all out to light the candles, nail mistletoe to the doorway, put on the music, and drape garlands on the banister, you just *have* to invite someone in to enjoy it all. You have to share the season, or it hardly seems worth celebrating at all.

One of my favorite moments during the holidays is when the cookies are baked, the tree is trimmed, the candles are lit, the fire is crackling, the music fills the house, and—TA-DA—you throw open the front door and welcome in your friends. Suddenly the place comes alive with laughter and chatter and hugs and kisses. Welcoming in a friend, or a few friends, or a whole bunch of friends through your front door is the one moment that best highlights Christmas joy.

Joy, you see, must be welcomed from the outside in.

That's the beauty of Christmas. It's appropriate that the Lord Jesus entered the inside of history from the outside. Joy came through a door when He crossed the threshold of this world to bring laughter and music into what was otherwise an empty, lonely place. Oh, sure, the world had all the trimmings, all the right props, all the tinsel. But it was only when Jesus entered in, that the world was filled with peace and joy.

Oswald Chambers has said, "The Lord came into history from the outside.... Jesus Christ is a being who cannot be accounted for by the human race at all. He is God incarnate, God coming into human flesh, coming into it from the outside. Our Lord's birth was an advent, a coming in. And just as our Lord came into human history from the outside, so He must come into me from the outside, as well."[1]

Paul had the same thing in mind when he expressed his fervent longing that Christ would be formed in his Galatian friends (Galatians 4:19). Until Christ was actually born in their hearts, the apostle felt like he was enduring the pains of childbirth!

So there you are, all dressed up in your Christmas best, waiting to share it with someone special. Well, the room will stay empty, lonely, and without music until you invite the Lord of Joy inside. It only happens when Christ is born in you, a "coming into"—much like swinging open the door to let Christmas begin.

Jesus stands outside the door of your holiday season. He wants to come in, to be born in you. Don't miss out on the best part of Christmas.

Open up and welcome Him in.

---

[1]Oswald Chambers, "Outside In" in *My Utmost for His Highest* (New York: Dodd, Mead & Co., 1935), 360.

THE LIFE OF A CHILD

Ah, the life of a child. To sleep peacefully, wrapped warm and cuddly in a soft blanket. Babies hardly have a care in the world. Hardly a worry in their little heads. Maybe that's because babies instinctively know that worries and cares are not their responsibility. After all, they know their mom will be there, tending to and caring for their every need. Such protection—relaxing in the confidence that they are safe from any harm. Such rest—assured that someone is always watching over them. No wonder they sleep so peacefully.

A child's life! Doesn't it make you a little envious? Don't you wish you could relax as easily, putting your worries and cares to rest? Wouldn't it be nice to have the confidence that someone was watching out for you, tending to your every need? Caring for you like a parent?

If that sounds good, it might be because you've got a lot of "adult" things pressing on you this Christmas season. You're anxious about picking up those last few gifts, you feel hassled and stretched by competing family demands, you're pressured to make it to that office party on time, you feel as if you're holding your family together like ribbon around a package. Or worse yet, perhaps you feel lonely or forgotten in the middle of all the festivities. Something dark or hurtful has shoved its way into your life, and peace of mind has slipped out a back window. You feel empty, hurt, or even rejected.

A child's life…doesn't sound so bad. Do you look at all those pictures of Jesus on the front of your Christmas cards—the ones of Him sleeping peacefully in His mother's arms—and think to yourself, "If only it were that easy. If only life were that simple"?

Maybe it is that simple.

Your loving heavenly Father hasn't forgotten His care for you, especially in the middle of all the Christmas rush, especially when you feel pressured and anxious. He still sees you as His child. He longs to wrap you tenderly in His care. You're protected by the strength of His arms, and He wants you to have confidence that you are safe in His will. Rest and relax in Him. He will never leave you. Sleep in peace tonight.

And if you feel far from Him right now, stop and take time to talk to Him—just like a child to a parent. It's Christmas, a good time to let all the wonder and delight of a child fill your heart.

As a child of God, you have every reason to be at peace.

WHITE AS SNOW

"Come now, let us reason together," says the Lord.
"Though your sins are like scarlet,
they shall be as white as snow;
though they are red as crimson,
they shall be like wool."

ISAIAH 1:18

I love snow. It can be dry, fast-falling flakes, or heavy, big ones that swirl and drift in the wind. It can be a few snowflakes that breeze by, or a blizzard that blasts in from the north. Whatever, I love to see the world turn white.

I remember one snowy afternoon when I was sitting by the window of our farmhouse, wishing I could jump out of my wheelchair and follow my sisters as they trekked through the drifts to the barn. They saddled their horses and came up the path to wave good-bye to me. I smiled and waved back, but inside I felt so hurt. I wanted to be out in the snow. I longed to feel it stick to my face and eyelashes.

I felt sorry for myself. But my sister Jay, after she came back at twilight from the horse-back ride, had just the remedy. After dinner she pushed me to the door, bundled a big blanket around me, and wrapped an afghan over my shoes. Pulling the blanket's edge up around my ears, Jay wheeled me outside onto the front patio of our farmhouse. It was dark, but the porch light illumined a thousand tiny flakes swirling and swishing in big circles.

Locking my wheelchair brakes, Jay asked if I felt comfortable. I nodded a nervous yes, and she smiled as she walked back into the house. After the door clicked shut, I sat and listened to the quiet. The quiet had a sound of its own, especially as I strained to listen to the soft, wet hiss of snow melting against the porch light.

A gentle wind whirled snow in little eddies across the patio, gathering flakes in the creases of my blanket. More snow drifted lightly around my wheels. I huffed and puffed, delighted to see frosty breath. I listened to the wind sigh through the pines lining the pasture. I breathed deep and felt the sting of icy air in my lungs, relishing the smell of a wood fire from the chimney.

Watching the world turn white cleaned away all my feelings of self-pity. Sadness vanished just like the ugly, muddy ruts in the pasture. No, I couldn't ride horseback through the drifts, but I could appreciate the pleasure of a snowy evening even while sitting still. Don't misunderstand. Accepting my wheelchair didn't happen right then and there. That evening was just one in a long series of many days when the Holy Spirit covered my hurt with His gentle grace.

This Christmas, what things are keeping you from appreciating God's pleasures? Do you resent your situation? Give the Lord an inch in your life, and He will take a mile, covering your scarlet sins as the snow outside your window covers the barren ground. Accepting your lot in life may not happen overnight, but today can be one in a series of many days when you find God taking your sin…and making your world as white as snow.

And don't you long for that?